Green Business, Social Responsibility, Organizational Ethics, and Nonprofit Organizations
4 Topics in 1 Book

Louis Bevoc

Published by
NutriNiche System LLC

Louis Bevoc books...simple explanations of complex subjects

Green
Business
The Role of Sustainability

Louis Bevoc

Published by
NutriNiche System LLC

Louis Bevoc books...simple explanations of complex subjects

Introduction

Green business is growing faster than it ever has in the past. It is an interesting concept because it focuses on minimizing rather than maximizing the impact of organizations. This way of thinking is perplexing to many business leaders because they are used to maximizing important areas of their organizations including income, sales, quality, and brand awareness. Their goal is to get the most "bang for their buck," and this is done be getting bigger and better.

Green business leaders are not of the "bigger and better" mentality. They strive to minimize the negative impact that their organizations have on society and the environment while becoming more transparent in their ongoing efforts for improvement. This is done by focusing on the triple-bottom line, a term first described by John Elkington in the mid-1990s, where profits are not based solely on income and sales. The environment and society are also taken into account and these factors, along with income and sales, make up the value of businesses and determine profitability.

The concept of the triple-bottom line needs further discussion in order to be fully understood...so let's move into that discussion.

Triple-bottom-line

Traditionally, the profitability (or the "bottom line") of business has been determined by profit and loss. Quite simply, expenses are subtracted from revenue and the difference is profitability. However, over the last half-century, this ideology has been challenged. Social scientists and environments believe profitability is defined by a much broader concept that takes society and the environment into account. Based on this thinking, they implemented a process where direct and indirect costs of financial, environmental, and social impacts are combined to determine what is known as the triple-bottom-line.

An example of a business adhering to the triple-bottom-line concept is a company that invests fifty percent of all profits back into the local community. This company employs refugees from war-torn nations who are assigned the responsibility of collecting metal scrap and recycling it for cash. Society benefits from the employment found for disadvantaged refugees, the local community benefits from the donations received, the environment benefits from the recycling, and the business benefits from the profits they keep. Essentially, everyone wins in what should be a long-term endeavor.

One major challenge associated with the triple-bottom line is that it can be difficult to accurately measure the value of the social and environmental impact. Green business is based on minimizing the negative impact, and this is difficult to gauge because the maximum impact of those negatives is unknown. This means some guesswork must be involved, and guesswork is frowned upon number-crunching people who prefer quantitative results supported by real data.

Hundreds of pages could be devoted to the concept of the triple-bottom line, but this book is not designed for that type of detail. It focuses on green business, and green business only requires a brief understanding of the triple-bottom line...which has now been provided.

Let's move on to the next section that focuses on sustainability as the key to the green business concept.

Sustainability

Sustainability is the thinking that everything people need is based on the natural environment, and they must find harmony with that environment in order to survive and thrive. One hand washes the other as humans and nature work to benefit each other. For example, people need to breathe air so they must make sure that air is kept clean for use. If that air is too polluted, then the future of humanity is at risk.

Many of the policies related to sustainability were established by environmentalists, but over time this thinking has become part of the mainstream. The United States made sustainability a national policy in 1969 by enacting the National Environmental Policy Act. This law allows the government to oversee environmental, social, and economic impact of human actions by implementing regulations, funding private projects, constructing public facilities, and managing the usage of land.

The branch of government responsible for establishing and enforcing rules and regulations related to sustainability is the Environmental Protection Agency (EPA). The EPA upholds this responsibility based on the following principles:

- *Protect and replenish natural resources related to water, land, air, and energy.*
- *Fund and support positive outcomes for environmental, social, and economic systems.*
- *Prevent and reduce waste, pollution, and contamination related to natural resources and the environment.*

Other nations have followed the general practices of sustainability for hundreds of years, even though most of them do not have writing policies that document their commitment. These nations' actions speak louder than their words, and some of those actions came about out of sheer necessity. For example, Europeans adhered to rules of environmental conservation because new that they could not exist without the resources that the earth provided. Those resources were renewable, but only if a plan was in place to make sure a conservation protocol was followed. Sustainability allowed people to live off the land and it assured that future generations could do the same.

Sustainability is often a misunderstood term in business. People confuse sustainability with social responsibility because both are concerned with society and the organization benefiting from the programs that are in place. However, there is a difference between these two terms because social responsibility focuses on the present, where sustainability is more about the future. For example, a lumber yard might feel a social responsibility to purchase all wood from nations with concern for human rights. However, from a sustainability standpoint, that same lumber yard might want to prevent the world's rain forests from being over-harvesting in order to protect them from becoming extinct. In short, social responsibility is geared toward short-term results while sustainability is concerned with long-term outcomes.

Sustainability is the crux of this book because green business is based it. In fact, sustainable business is often called green business because the latter term is more easily understood. People are familiar with the term "green" because the environment is at the forefront of many discussions today. Global warming is an example of a green topic that is familiar to people all over the world. The real impact of global warming is sometimes a hot topic of debate, but it cannot be ignored by companies that want to be labeled as green businesses.

There is no absolute definition of green business because all businesses are different and they are all impacted by unique variables. However, in general, businesses are considered green if they meet the following two criteria:

- *Principles of sustainability are incorporated into all major decisions.*

  This indicates the business is committed to minimizing negative impact on people and the environment while preserving and replenishing natural resources. For example, a dental practice decides to use only mercury-free materials for tooth fillings; thereby reducing the chance that mercury will slowly seep into people's bloodstreams causing health damage. This change benefits people living today, and it offers future generations an opportunity for healthier living.

- *Products or services offered by the business replace non-green products and services offered by other businesses.*

  This indicates the business is meeting an established demand rather than a new demand; thereby minimizing the negative impact on the environment. For example, a cleaning company introduces a hand soap that is completely biodegradable. This product replaces hand soaps with non-biodegradable ingredients, so contaminants do not enter the sewer systems and natural sources of water are kept cleaner now and for future generations.

In the above examples, the dental firm and cleaning company attempt to positively impact the future of humans and the environment by making changes. These changes meet the needs of people today without compromising the needs of future generations. The materials used for the fillings and the hand soap are renewable, so both organizations meet the definition of a green business. Ideally, consumers are willing to pay more money for both of these products because they believe in the green concept, so the companies benefit financially.

A simple way to think about green business is the analogy of a rocket that requires three different engines to propel it into space. The first engine is made up of the people in society, the second engine is made up of the environment and the natural resources within it, and the third engine is the financial well-being of the business itself. All three engines need to be operating simultaneously in order move forward with green ideas and concepts. When the engines run in unison, harmony is achieved and sustainability works to reduce the negative impacts on society, the environment, and the profitability of the organization. In short, a positive triple bottom line is achieved.

Green businesses create value for everyone involved. Customers, suppliers, employees, investors, and society all benefit from the positive effects...now and in the future. The following exemplifies these benefits using an agricultural business:

> Couples & Barth is a fishery in Maine that farm raises trout for sale to supermarkets all over the region. They use environmentally friendly methods of farming that allow them to produce fish while minimizing the negative impact on people and the environment. For example, they use solar panels to produce 20 percent of the energy required to run the farm. They also use natural cleaning compounds rather than chemicals to clean the water in their ponds.

The green efforts of Couples & Barth are beneficial to people and the environment. The solar panels conserve energy and minimize the depletion of natural resources; thereby allowing those resources to be used by future generations of people. The natural cleaning compounds keep water in the ponds clean while doing minimal damage to the surrounding soil and earth. There is less pollution and soil erosion, which benefits current and future generations of people living in the surrounding area.

The fact that Couples & Barth operate as a green business allows them to charge higher prices and sell more trout than their competition. Customers are happy to support the cause because they know they are helping people and the environment. Additionally, the higher sales volume creates jobs at the farm in order to keep up with the product demand, and the company is financially healthy due to increased profitability.

Couples & Barth is an organization that fits the definition of a green business. They are committed to minimizing negative impact on the environment by preserving and replenishing natural resources and providing a product that meets the needs of an established market. They survive and thrive by finding true harmony with the environment, and their actions allow them to have a positive triple-bottom-line.

Couples & Barth is an example of a green business that works, but a green business in agriculture is different from those in other industries. Every green organization must tailor their processes and procedures to meet specific needs while showing concern for people and the environment. However, there are some common strategies that all organizations can use to achieve the valued green status...and those strategies are discussed in the next section.

Common strategies

Businesses need strategies in order to become green and maintain their green status. If these strategies are not in place, then there is nothing to separate them from other businesses that provide the same products or services.

One common misconception about green strategies is that they cost more money than they are worth. Leaders who think this way simply do not understand the green concept, and they should not attempt to make their businesses green before developing that understanding. Green strategies actually save money because they take advantage of opportunities available for cost reduction. They protect businesses from violating regulatory environmental requirements, conserve resources, and save on energy-related expenses. For example, many industrial facilities pay surcharges based on the contaminants they discharge into their sewer systems. Environmentally friendly companies can replace some of the chemicals used in their facilities with natural compounds, thereby resulting in cleaner sewage discharge and lower surcharge costs. Another example is a company that turns wind into energy. Large windmills are turned by air to create power for their operations; thereby saving on energy costs that would be incurred using electricity or natural gas.

Some common strategies from green businesses are listed below. These strategies are quite simple, but they provide a framework for implementation and maintenance of green concepts.

Establish goals

A goal is usually the end result of a strategy, but establishing that goal requires a strategy of its own. Green thinking must be behind all decision-making related to goals even though it is easy to get out of that mindset due to cost, implementation, or maintenance reasons. For example, a green manufacturing company might have a goal of paying every employee at least 40 percent more than the minimum wage established by the government. This benefits humans because workers are assured that they will earn a livable wage.

Continuous improvement

Essentially, this is the ongoing process of continually improving the products and services being offered by the organization. For green businesses, this means continually evaluating their products or services and making changes that benefit the environment of society. For example, a lawn care company that donates 50 percent of all profits to groups working to conserve natural resources might improve by requiring all lawns to be mowed with electric lawnmowers. This minimizes pollution; thereby benefitting the environment.

Teamwork

Most people who have worked in business understand that teamwork is necessary to accomplish objectives. However, green teamwork involves collaboration with the entire supply chain in order to benefit people or the environment. For example, a computer manufacturer that uses all recycled or refurbished components might collaborate with a distributor to produce webinars that show the benefits of green computers from an environmental standpoint.

Creativity

In many ways, creativity is similar to continuous improvement because companies use it to get better. However, green businesses must be creative in order to survive because they compete for a portion of a relatively small market. This creativity typically comes in the form of innovation, often using technology as the cornerstone. For example, a green pastry manufacturer might discover a new all natural preservative that can be used to extend the shelf life of their products. In this instance, the pastry company is improving itself...but that improvement was only possible because research and development people used modern technology to make a hybrid of natural ingredients that works to preserve food.

As noted in the beginning of this section, the strategies above are simple. There is no rocket-science involved with any of these methods for moving forward, but they need to be utilized if businesses want to achieve a true green status. The next section shows the importance of this status based on the influence it has on decision making in organizations.

Paving the way

Like it or not, green concepts and ideas impact decisions made by business leaders. They are forced to take green thinking into consideration because people all over the world are concerned about society and the environment. This is not to say that companies are completely committing to going green...it simply means that if they choose to ignore people and the environment, then they risk losing a part of their customer base.

Slowly but surely, business leaders are realizing the importance of becoming environmentally-friendly. They understand the upfront costs will be recouped over time via the triple-bottom line even though they are competing with non-green organizations that do not need to meet the same requirements. Based on their actions, business leaders understand that green thinking leads to good decision-making for their organizations.

One particular aspect of green business that cannot be ignored is the fact that it stimulates a wealth of debate regarding its role, importance, and impact. There is always disagreement due to fear, uncertainty, misunderstanding, or resentment. Opponents of the green revolution see no real value in it and often do not believe the arguments for its implementation. They regard data presented by defenders of the environment as made up hype that is designed to scare people into jumping on the green bandwagon. They also believe the cost of green must be passed on to the customers, and those customers simply will not pay the additional price. However, based on consumer love for society for the environment, naysayer business leaders have little choice other than to become socially responsible or they risk losing a segment of their customer base.

Regardless of what business leaders believe, it is a fact that some green technology lowers costs. Examples abound in terms of energy usage. Wind and solar power are essentially free after the initial set up costs, and this provides cost savings to the organizations that choose to utilize these energy forms. This savings shows in the triple-bottom line, but it also shows also shows in the traditional bottom line...a feat that some people did not think was possible when going green.

Green concepts are paving the way to a new type of thinking. Despite the challenges involved, business leaders realize the added value of green products and services. This realization is accomplished by changing of mindsets. In short, business leaders view green business in a positive light by altering their perception as follows:

Customers prefer green products and services

This is likely the easiest perception to change because the facts speak for themselves. In the past, business leaders did not think customers wanted anything to do with green products or services, and they were probably right. However, times have changed and consumers are much more conscious about acting now to preserve the environment for future generations. The earth and the people who inhabit it are now at the forefront of consumer concerns, and their purchases are quite indicative of this change in thinking.

Astute business leaders have a goal of growing their organizations' sales. They watch their markets intensely and react as quickly as possible when trends develop. They see the trend of green products and services, and this has changed their perception of the green concept. "Go green" is now part of a marketing plan rather than an obscure thought.

Obstacles are seen as opportunities

This is likely the hardest perception to change because it involves a complete reversal of thinking. In general, most people think of obstacles as roadblocks that must be removed in order to move forward. They spend a lot of time trying to figure how to eliminate these roadblocks and ultimately end up giving up or navigating around them in order to reach their destination. Either way, they lose something because giving up is failure and navigating around something results in making sacrifices that often do not justify the achievement.

Sharp business leaders view obstacles as opportunities to improve, and that perception works well for green business. For example, a meat processing plant might have to comply with an EPA rule that requires their smokehouse to emit 25 percent less pollution within the three years. They can purchase a $20,000 air scrubber that will reduce the pollution by the required 25 percent. However, they can also purchase a $35,000 air scrubber that will reduce 60 percent of the pollution. They view the $35,000 air scrubber as an opportunity to better themselves because it will exceed EPA standards and it will also reduce the complaints from neighborhood residents who have found the smoke to be an annoyance. They purchase the more expense scrubber even though it is tempting to adhere to the lowest environmental standards due to cost reasons.

Regulations drive the supply chain

Traditionally, leaders of companies that supply products and services to consumers have viewed regulations a necessary cost of doing business. They conform because they are required to do so, and they absorb 100 percent of the costs in the process. However, green rules and regulations affect the entire supply chain....not just the businesses supplying the products or services.

Smart business leaders know that green regulations are not limited to their own organizations. They understand that the rules are mandatory for every company in the supply chain, from suppliers to customers, so they all need to make changes. Their mindset of making changes "because we have to" goes out the window, and their new perception is that every company is making changes to better the entire chain. It is a team effort, and every organization shares some of the responsibility; thereby lifting the sole burden off the companies that supply products and services to consumers.

Triple-bottom lines are important

Traditional bottom lines based on profitability will always be indicators of business success. Investors, stockholders, and employees view profitability as a sign of organizational health...and they make decisions to invest in or work for those organizations based on that view. This is the way it was in the past, the way it is now, and the way it will be in future. However, green business has added a new dimension to this old thinking with the introduction of the triple-bottom line. The triple-bottom-line takes society and the environment into account because customers are demanding more green products and services than they ever have in the past. Profitability needs to be determined based on that demand, and the traditional bottom lines do not show the entire picture.

There is little doubt that green businesses will pave the way for the future. They will continue to grow as organizations all over the world realize the importance of preserving the environment and improving human lives. A constant stream of new green ideas and concepts are being generated today, and this trend will continue as more money is spent funding green research with the expectation that the investment will be recouped over time.

Now, let's move on to the next section that suggests specific actions that businesses can take to assure the environment is better for future generations.

Reducing carbon footprints

A major goal of any green business is to decrease the damage that their products and services do to people and the environment. One method of evaluating that damage involves measuring the amount of carbon produced by an organization. Essentially, this is done by measuring greenhouse gases (gases that keep heat from exiting the atmosphere of the earth) produced by the organization....more commonly known as measuring that organization's carbon footprint.

The term "carbon footprint" is understood by many people regardless of their experience with green business. They know the term refers to an individual or organization's impact on the environment, even though they are unsure of the exact definition. For the purposes of this book, the carbon footprint of business is defined as:

The amount of carbon dioxide emitted by an organization that uses fossil fuels

High levels of carbon dioxide are not good for people because it can adversely affect respiratory functions in the body by displacing oxygen in the air. Based on this fact, it is rather obvious that carbon dioxide emission needs to be minimalized...and that is why this section focuses on reduction of carbon footprints.

Fossil fuels are non-renewable sources of energy that leave a carbon footprint when burned. Unfortunately, many different types of businesses burn large amounts of fossil fuels when they operate. Vehicles, machinery, refrigeration, and heating all require energy...and that energy typically comes from fossil fuels. That being said, the following are some ways to reduce carbon footprints in business:

Paperless communication

This involves sending electronic correspondence instead of paper. It saves money by not having to buy the paper and ink necessary for writing. More importantly, it eliminates the energy required to distribute paper, and it saves the fossils fuels burned during the manufacturing process.

Telecommuting is a type of paperless communication that deserves mention due to its growing popularity. It is valuable for the environment because it reduces energy usage and creates a happier workforce because employees can work from just about anywhere that has internet access.

In general, paperless communication works well for reducing the carbon footprint of businesses. The minimized environmental impact and cost savings truly make it an opportunity rather than an obstacle for achieving green status.

Recycle

This refers to reusing a product rather than making it new at the expense of the environment. That expense is more complex than it might appear because it is more than just the energy needed for manufacturing. It also includes the energy needed to transport the old item to a landfill, the pollution that results from the transfer of that old item, the landfill space required to bury the old item, and the impact on the environment if the old item is not readily biodegradable. The carbon footprint expands with each step of the process, and it can be prevented with simple recycling.

Businesses need comprehensive recycling policies in place that include exploring new options because the entire world is thinking and acting greener than it ever has in the past. Consumers are demanding green products and services, and businesses need to react in a timely and efficient manner in order to meet those demands.

Product and process design

Product design is important because, when done properly, it eliminates waste and reduces the negative effects on the environment. For example, a rubber toy might need to have the excess rubber trimmed off after it comes out of a mold. That mold can be redesigned to minimize the waste that is trimmed. That same toy could also incorporate more environmentally friendly raw materials so it breaks down faster after it meets its final resting place in a landfill.

Processes can also be redesigned to be more environmentally friendly. Waste can be eliminated by changing the way products are made and incorporating rework back into those products. For example, a confectionary can implement a process to rework scrap candy into new batches of the same product. Additionally, the lines for packing that candy can be redesigned so fewer pieces fall on the floor and end up being disposed of in the trash.

One last aspect of product process and design that needs to be discussed involves procedures. Procedures for energy conservation need to be updated to meet the needs of green business. Lights, machines, and equipment must be turned off when they are not in use. These conservative practices are easy ways to reduce carbon footprints, but they are often ignored because employees are not in the habit of taking the appropriate action. However, they will change their habits and think about energy conservation if they are constantly reminded to do so via new procedures.

In short, businesses can reduce their carbon footprints by designing their products and processes so they utilize renewable resources and have a minimum negative impact on the environment. They need to take consumer concerns into account and make decisions with the entire product life cycle in mind. This incorporates a "recycle, rework, and reuse" mentality while thinking about energy usage, government regulations, processing, storage, and disposal. In other words, business must consider the impact on nature from cradle-to-grave.

Avoid greenwashing

Although greenwashing is not necessarily a way to reduce carbon footprints, it needs to be mentioned because it is harmful to society and the environment. Greenwashing is a deceptive practice where organizations promote themselves as being environmentally friendly when this is not really true.

Businesses that engage in greenwashing are deceptive because they are doing more damage to the environment than they admit. An example is a company that promotes a cleaning product as all natural when, in fact, it contains some chemicals. This type of behavior makes consumers distrust the entire green industry, and it reduces their desire to make green products and services the norm.

In short, greenwashing is fraudulent activity that is environmentally destructive and leads to people believing something that is not legitimate or true. This practice needs to be avoided, or carbon footprints will increase without any type of resistance.

Summary

Green business minimizes the negative impact of organizations on society and the environment. It makes businesses stronger by focusing on the triple-bottom line that takes nature into account in addition to income and sales.

This book explores green business as it relates society and the environment. It examines the triple-bottom line, recommends common strategies for implementation and maintenance, discusses the impact on decisions of business leaders, and suggests methods for reducing carbon footprints. The text is educational and informational, and it is written for easy reader understanding at all levels.

Congratulations! You now understand more about green business....and increasingly important concept for organizations all over the world.

Social Responsibility
of Organizations
Explaining and Understanding

Louis Bevoc

Published by
NutriNiche System LLC

Louis Bevoc books...simple explanations of complex subjects

Introduction

Social responsibility is an obligation to act in ways that benefit society. For organizations, this means the stakeholders (people with have an interest in the organization's success) must make sure that there is a balance between their economy and the environment. In other words, profitability is not the only concern.

Some people in business find it difficult to put any aspect of business on the same level as financial success. After all, money drives organizations because, without it, those organizations would cease to exist. However, it has been suggested that social responsibility leads to profitability because many socially responsible thoughts and ideas are generated by the public...and companies that ignore those thoughts and ideas have difficulty selling their products and services.

Organizations become socially responsible by behaving in one of two ways. The first way involves internal actions that make sure the organization or the people in it do not engage in any type of socially harmful actions. An example is a foundry that invites the EPA to inspect the soil on their property for contamination that might harm the environment. This inspection is not required, but it goes "above and beyond" to protect the environment. The second way involves external actions that do something to directly advance socially responsible goals and objectives. An example is an oil company that invests money, time, and effort in wildlife preservation activities. They did not do any damage to the wildlife that they are working toward preserving, but they want to show that they are concerned about the environment and take appropriate action to highlight that concern.

Now that you understand a little bit about the social responsibility of organizations, we need to move into a discussion on classification. This is done in the next section that identifies the major types of social responsibility.

Types

In the early 1990's, Archie Carroll developed a socially responsible pyramid that defined four basic corporate responsibilities. This pyramid has basic stakeholder responsibilities at the bottom (legal and economic) and higher societal responsibilities (ethical and philanthropic) at the top. Similar to Abraham Maslow's *Hierarchy of Needs*, lower-level responsibilities of organizations must be met before moving on to the responsibilities that benefit society.

For this book, the social responsibilities of Carroll's pyramid are listed separately without regard to the importance of progression. An additional responsibility that addresses volunteering has also been added for better understanding. That being said, the types of social responsibilities discussed in this book are as follows:

Economic

This is probably the most well-known type of social responsibility, and it refers to an organization's responsibilities to its stakeholders. Businesses are obligated to create jobs, offer valuable products and services, and provide a return-on-investment to stockholders and investors. Organizations must also operate as effectively and efficiently as possible while offering innovative products and services. Most business leaders understand this type of social responsibility and make it one of their top priorities because it helps grow their organizations and sustain their livelihoods.

An example of economic social responsibility is a grocery store chain that enters the high end market of organic foods. They know organic items are very trendy and profitable, and selling them will positively impact their bottom line. This keeps the company healthy and makes shareholders happy.

Ethical

This type of social responsibility is growing in importance. Organizations are held accountable for the ways they treat the environment, employees, suppliers, customers, and the general public. They are expected to recycle, properly dispose of waste, be fair to their employees, and be truthful to customers about products or services. They are also expected not to play favorites due friendships, family relationships, or romances. In short, this responsibility involves refraining from behavior that is questionable even though it is not necessarily illegal and acting responsibility in all situations. Sometimes this means going above and beyond what is required by the law.

An example of ethical social responsibility is an accounting firm that offers paid maternity leave to men and women. This is not required by law, but it is an ethical action that allows parents to spend time with newborn babies without worrying about finances. This shows that the company respects their employees and is concerned about their happiness and well-being.

Legal

Legal social responsibilities cannot be ignored because they are required by law. Organizations need to obey all laws established by the government. Government agencies that enforce laws include the Internal Revenue Service (IRS), Occupational Safety and Health Administration (OSHA), National Labor Relations Board (NLRB), and the Securities and Exchange Commission (SEC).

An example of legal social responsibility is a pawn shop that keeps accurate track of all cash sales as required by law. Cash transactions can be difficult for the IRS to verify, so the pawn shop makes sure these sales are transparent to avoid scrutiny or an audit. They make sure they adhere to the law by doing the right thing.

Philanthropic

This type of social responsibility involves promoting causes that organizations believe are justifiable. It is typically done by giving money in the form of donations, but it can also be in the form of services. Either way, the giving reflects well on the perception of organizations because they are viewed as being charitable.

An example of philanthropic social responsibility is an automotive supplier matching 100 percent of employee monetary donations to the St. Jude Children's Hospital. This action shows compassion and is for a good cause. It also encourages employees to donate by making them feel that their donations are important.

Volunteer

Volunteer social responsibilities do not involve the direct giving of money. Instead, employees offer their services for something that their employer believes is justifiable. This reflects well on the perception of organizations, and it gets people personally involved in a good cause.

An example of volunteer social responsibility is a pharmaceutical company that recruits its employees to work at local soup kitchens. This action shows compassion for those who are less fortunate and it benefits the community. It also benefits the employees because they feel like they are doing something good for the community.

Now you understand the basic types of social responsibility for organizations. Next, let's move into the impact of social responsibility.

Impact

Social responsibility impacts organizations in many different ways. It affects employees, customers, suppliers, and the public in positive and negative ways depending on individual perception of the situation. Some people are very concerned about social responsibility, while others rarely think about it. However, it is important because it can affect the bottom line...and the bottom line is important to every business.

The following are directly impacted by the social responsibility of organizations:

Customers

This refers to the retention of current customers and the acquisitions of new ones. Some people simply will not buy products or services from organizations that they do not believe are socially responsible. Instead, they patronize businesses that share similar values.

This type of impact can have a "trickle-down" effect that goes quite deep. For example, a person might refuse to eat at a restaurant because the chicken that restaurant sells comes from a farm that raises birds in cages rather them letting them live "free range" style. This action directly impacts the restaurant, but it also indirectly affects the distributor that delivers the chicken, the processor that prepares the chicken, the slaughterhouse that kills the chicken, and the farmer that raises chicken. In this case, the impact of the person's action is much deeper than it might appear on the surface.

Investment

Investors are needed by many companies, and social responsibility affects those investors. This affect can be positive or negative, depending on perception. For example, an investor might be looking for a company to put money into that is concerned about the environment. They will not invest in a business that is socially irresponsible in terms of the ecosystem....regardless of the potential for return-on-investment.

Like it or not, entire communities are sometimes affected by investment decisions. Small towns rely on businesses to support their economies because those businesses create jobs and generate tax revenue. If a company falls short of receiving an investment due to their inability to be socially responsible, then they can damage the financial well-being of many people who have nothing in common with that company other than to live in the same community.

Image

Every marketing professor knows the importance of image. In their minds, image makes or breaks organizations. Like it or not, social responsibility affects the image of companies all over the world. For example, "sweat shops" in other nations that employ people at very low wages are frowned upon by people who are concerned about human rights and violations of ethical social responsibility. Along the same lines, an embezzlement scandal makes a financial institution look bad due to a disregard for economic social responsibility. In short, social responsibility forms images of organizations in people's minds...and a negative image can be very difficult to change.

An example of a negative image is a pharmaceutical company that keeps prices high on drugs that people need to survive so shareholders can profit immensely. This company has little concern for the individuals who need their medication, and the public perceives it as having an image of being uncaring and greedy. This image will be hard to change even if the company takes steps to replace economic social responsibility with ethical social responsibility.

Recruitment

As noted above, social responsibility is directly related to image. That image is engrained in people's minds, and it is hard to alter. That image also drives the recruitment process because organizations with positive images are attractive to some potential employees. For example, younger employees often place a high importance on the ecosystem. They prefer to work for organizations that are environmentally socially responsible, and they will not consider employment with companies that have little regard for the environment.

Recruitment is influenced by social responsibility of organizations more than many people realize. This is because some people's thinking is subliminal based on the values they have had in place since childhood. They instinctively react to situations based on their values, and this will not change unless their self-awareness is modified by some type of external stimuli or source.

Goals

Social responsibility is important for the establishment of goals and objectives. For example, if leaders of an organization have a goal of making a difference in society, they can achieve it using philanthropic social responsibility. They simply pick a charitable organization and give money to it while encouraging their employees to donate. In this regard, social responsibility encourages organizations to get better and look better in the eyes of outsiders.

Conflict

As some people have likely experienced, social responsibility can create warring factions in organizations. This is due to the fact that the people involved with the specific types of social responsibility are not of the same mindset. For example, economic social responsibility puts profitability above everything else; which does not work well for those concerned with ethical or philanthropic social responsibility. This creates conflict and, unfortunately, that conflict can become dysfunctional. Dysfunctional conflict is destructive because position becomes more important than principle...and then people are attacked instead of the problem. These personal attacks are always negative, and nothing constructive gets accomplished. In short, the tension resulting from different types of social responsibility leads to dysfunctional conflict and long-lasting problems that are difficult to resolve.

Now you understand the impact that social responsibility has on various aspects of organizations. Let's move on to discussing the advantages and disadvantages social responsibility provides organizations...starting with the advantages.

Advantages

Social responsibility provides benefits for organizations. This should not come as a surprise, but most people do not realize these benefits because they associate social responsibility with increased costs. Sometimes this is true, but certain companies become more profitable by being socially responsible because the changes they undergo project a more positive image to stakeholders and the public. That being said, the major advantages of social responsibility are as follows:

Reputation

There is an old saying that reputation follows people wherever they go. This saying is also true for organizations...but it needs to be expanded upon because, after a while, reputation progresses from a following to a leading role. It leads some companies to growth and prosperity, while it leads others to their graves.

Social responsibility establishes reputations because people see and hear things that influence their thinking. If they see a company donate to charity on a regular basis, then they think highly of that organization. On the other hand, if they see a company where greed drives executives at the expense of others, then they think negatively about that organization.

In short, reputation is an important part of perception that is driven by social responsibility. Organizations that realize this importance find their social responsible actions advantageous because they are viewed in a positive light by others.

Customer relationships

Socially responsible organizations build good relationships internally and externally. They establish a rapport with the charities they support, understand the needs of their stakeholders, and work well with the government agencies that regulate their actions.   These relationships help build trust with customers because those customers understand the organizations they purchase suppliers and services from are legally, ethically, and economically responsible. Trust leads to the loyalty necessary for repeat business, and it prevents customers from looking for new companies to buy from just because they are less expensive. In short, social responsibility is advantageous because it helps establish and maintain solid customer relationships.

Compliance

Legal social responsibility is great for keeping organizations in compliance with rules and regulations. This is critical because violations cost money, and they can completely stop companies from operating. When companies are compliant, their efficiency also improves so managers can focus on doing their jobs rather than dealing with enforcement officers or auditors.

Compliance also reduces worry because there is no concern that regulatory actions could be around the corner. This is a significant benefit because worry leads to stress...and stress causes employees to burn out. In the long run, morale is increased, turnover is reduced, and the knowledge employees have acquired remains with their organizations.

Innovation

Innovation is necessary for the growth and prosperity of organizations. This innovation does not necessarily have to be cutting edge, but it needs to be present in some form. Innovation takes companies to the next level using new concepts and ideas, and it tends to snowball once it begins.

Social responsibility helps organizations become more innovative. It does this by forcing people to move outside of their comfort zones and still meet goals....often in ways that were never previously considered. For example, in the 1970s, the government forced automobile manufacturers to meet new fuel economy standards. Engineers started working on reducing the weight of cars so they would require less gas to operate. This led to the development of stronger, lighter, and more flexible materials that helped meet the new standards. However, an added plus was that these materials were also cheaper, which lead to a cost saving that was previously unrealized.

Planning

At first glance, this might not appear to be an advantage. After all, planning in organizations should occur regardless of whether or not socially responsible actions are taking place. However, social responsibility promotes long-term planning because it forces leaders to think about the future so they can maintain their current status. They need to think strategically about ways to incorporate socially responsible actions into the long-term growth of their organizations. This prevents them from focusing only on the short-term goals, such as profitability and return-on-investment, that are most important to investors and stock holders...and it benefits their organizations as a whole because a variety of different factors are taken into consideration.

Now you understand some of the advantages related to the social responsibility of organizations. However, a fair analysis needs to include some of the negatives that are also involved...and those negatives are discussed in the next section.

Problems

Some people argue that the time, money, and effort spent by organizations trying to become socially responsible is not worth it. Quite simply, they believe the negatives outweigh the positives...and this will not change. This section explores those negatives by discussing the following problems associated with social responsibility:

Competition

Social responsibility often requires organizations to change employee mindsets about how business is conducted because self-imposed rules and regulations restrict some options. The resulting lack of freedom is not felt by the competitors of these organizations, and it gives those competitors an advantage selling products or services. In short, social responsibility can cause organizations to lose their increasingly important competitive edge.

Cost

There is a cost associated with social responsibility, and that cost can get out of hand if it is not monitored closely. Programs designed to reduce environmental destruction though ethical practices or prevent disease through philanthropic actions can be expensive with no real way to recoup the money spent. This can cause companies a variety of different problem including the inability to meet financial obligations.

This type of problem can have a huge impact on small companies with limited financial resources. They need money in more important areas of their businesses so they can continue to operate, even though their customers and the public might believe otherwise.

Stockholders

This problem expands on the cost issue, and it might be the most common negatives associated with social responsibility. Organizations have a fiduciary obligation to watch out for the best interests of stockholders, and that obligation is sometimes tossed aside in favor of social responsibility. Stockholders usually buy stock in a company because they want to earn income on the money they have invested. They want a return-on-investment (ROI), and that ROI is hindered by social responsibility because it does not produce income...at least in the short-term. In fact, some types of social responsibility, such as charitable donations, never generate income that can be readily seen. There are tax deductions for these types of financial transactions, but their impact on the bottom line is typically not good.

Not surprisingly, stockholders are often the most vocal opponents of social responsibility. They do not like seeing money come out of their pockets and put into something that might or might not be beneficial. Unfortunately, this issue will likely never go away as long as organizations continue to spend money on socially responsible actions.

Greenwashing

Without a doubt, greenwashing is unethical...and it also borders being illegal. As noted in the shareholder section, organizations have a fiduciary responsibility to stockholders. If the stock does not perform, then someone needs to be held accountable. Often times that person is the top decision maker also known as the CEO.

Because CEO's jobs are based on company performance, they sometimes allow for false or misleading information to be released or assumed. When the environment is involved, the release of false or misleading information is known as greenwashing. In short, greenwashing refers to organizations that claim to conduct business practices that are environmentally friendly or ethical when this is not really true.

Greenwashing is best understood using the following examples:

- A meat processer claims to buy meat that is humanely slaughtered, and they have a certificate to prove it. This is true...when the processor buys meat from a specific slaughterhouse because that slaughterhouse has a third-party audit conducted on a yearly basis to certify their humane processes. However, the meat processer fails to make consumers aware of the fact that over 70 percent of the meat they purchase is from other non-certified slaughterhouses. This meat is bought from local distributors who obtain meat that was slaughtered overseas in ways not considered to be humane.
- A mutual fund company claims to be green because they no longer send out paper brochures. Instead, prospective customers can access a website with information on every fund offered. However, the company is not even close to being completely green because they still send out privacy policies, account statements, tax forms, change notices, and voting ballets in paper form.
- A grocery store claims to be green because all packaging materials used in their deli are recyclable. This is true, but they fail to mention that 80 percent of the plastic products used in their bakery and produce departments are non-recyclable and add to the waste in landfills.

The internet provides an easy way to point out companies that greenwash, and this can turn customers off to their products or services. In short, partial truthfulness about social responsibility often ends up hurting businesses rather than helping them.

Groupthink

This disadvantage is saved for last because it is the most interesting. Psychologist Irving Janis established the term "Groupthink" to describe a process in which a group can make irrational decisions. In these situations, group members attempt to conform to what they believe to be the consensus of the group. The end result is the group ultimately agreeing on something that each member might normally view as unwise. This defeats the entire purpose of team decision making in organizations because ideas are stymied and synergy is virtually non-existent.

Groupthink causes two different and opposite problems. The first problem involves companies becoming too engrossed in social responsibility. For example, the CEO of a bank holds a meeting with all vice presidents to discuss social responsibility of the organization. The CEO strongly believes the bank needs to give more money to charities, and she suggests giving $1,000,000 to breast cancer research. This seems excessive to many the vice presidents...especially since the bank already gives over $300,000 annually to other charities. However, none of the vice presidents speak up or disagree. In fact, they all state that this is a good idea because they do not want to offend the CEO or the other vice presidents. They unanimously agree to donate the breast cancer research money, and the meeting adjourns.

In reality, the bank is very socially responsible because they already give generously to charity. The vice presidents agreed to the $1,000,000 breast cancer research donation even though many of them thought it was unnecessary and excessive. They conformed to what they believed was the consensus of the CEO and the other vice presidents, thereby destroying the benefits of group synergy. In this situation, the bank is too engrossed in social responsibility and they could jeopardize their financial well-being with their actions.

The second problem occurs when groupthink causes companies to not do enough in terms of social responsibility. For example, managers of a restaurant chain meet at the headquarters to evaluate the social responsibility of the organization. Each manager is afraid to express their personal beliefs because they fear it will offend other managers. Instead, every person in the meeting indicates that the restaurant chain is doing enough in terms of social responsibility because they believe that is what everyone wants to hear. They all agree that nothing else needs to be done, and the meeting adjourns.

In reality, the restaurant chain is doing very little to address social responsibility. The managers agreed that that enough was being done even though some of them thought differently. They conformed to what they believed was the consensus of management, thereby destroying the benefits of synergy that typically come from group decision making. In other words, the meeting did nothing to evaluate the social responsibility of the restaurant chain other than reducing it to an insignificant factor. In this situation, the restaurant chain is not doing enough in terms of social responsibility.

Now you understand some of the more important negatives associated with social responsibility. Based on these, it is understandable that companies can get better...and that leads us to the next section on improving social responsibility.

Improving

The reality of organizational social responsibility is that it has the potential to backfire and it is not accepted by everyone. Based on this, it is rather obvious that there is room for improvement. Although this improvement will not solve every problem, it will help gain acceptance of the responsibilities that companies maintain. That being said, the following are ways to improve the social responsibility of organizations:

Invent

Organizations need to be more innovative in terms of social responsibility. They must come up with ways to get better instead of waiting to be told what they need to do. For example, an oil company could contribute to charitable organizations that help wildlife after their habitat has been destroyed. This must be done before, not after, the company has their own oil spill to show that they have invented a way to reach out to the community without being in an emergency situation. This action will reflect well on the oil company if they make a mistake and damage the environment in the future. In short, organizations must be proactive instead of reactive in order to improve their social responsibility.

Invest

Most good things in life require some sort of investment…and this is certainly true for the social responsibility of organizations. Resources need to be allocated for an ongoing effort to maintain and improve social responsibility. For example, employees can be designated to develop strategies and designate funding for projects that make sure workers find job satisfaction. This falls under ethical social responsibility, and it prevents future problems by addressing issues before they fester into something bigger. In short, a little time and money spent now can prevent a lot of time and money from being spent later on.

Lead

Astute leaders hold themselves accountable for all organizational actions regardless of the nature of those actions. In terms of social responsibility, leaders need to have a vision and hold themselves accountable for making sure employees are working toward that vision. This requires delegation and monitoring to make sure tasks are getting completed. For example, a leader might have a vision of eliminating all unethical behavior of management. A goal of zero tolerance for bribery from vendors is established, and it is monitored with quarterly audits designed to look for potential occurrences of any type of unethical payoff. In short, leaders need to establish a vision and make sure employees are doing the things necessary to reach the goals related to that vision.

Listen

This method for improvement is often not given the credit it deserves. Leaders in organizations need to listen to the things people are saying about their organizations. Many times this can only be done by asking because people because they do not always volunteer information. For example, a chemical company that generates unpleasant smells could analyze the effects they have on the environment by listening to local residents. The information received could be used to develop systems that reduce the most offensive smells. Along the same lines, the company could also institute a community program that educates the local residents about these odors and their effects. These actions create an ongoing dialog with local folks, and they all stem from listening to the concerns of people.

The key to listening is communication. Organizations need communicate with people to determine the things that need to be done in terms of social responsibility. Listening leads to ideas that can prevent a wealth of problems down the line.

Now you are aware of ways that social responsibility can be improved...but this raises a question. What will social responsibility entail in the future? The answer is found in the next section.

Future

To be quite honest, the future of social responsibility is somewhat uncertain. There will always be challenges, and leaders of organizations will need to decide if they want to meet those challenges. However, it is rather clear that in the future more committees and teams will be formed to address social responsibility. These committees and teams will be charged with making decisions that involve:

Information

This refers to the release of information the public. Too little information can make it appear as if something is being hidden, and too much information can lead to unnecessary problems. For example, a fishing boat might spill 10 gallons of oil into the ocean. Should this information be released to the public? Ethically speaking, the owner of the shipping boat has an obligation to report the spill. However, a report of this nature might spark public outcry or a government investigation over 10 gallons of oil spilled into a massive ocean. In the future, organizations will be forced with decisions regarding the amount of information that needs to be released...and this will present some challenges.

Community

Organizations, especially those that are large, will need to get involved in the community in order to be socially responsible. This could involve donations to local charities, volunteering to help local folks in need, or working on projects for the environment. Regardless of the method of action chosen, leaders of organizations will increasingly realize the value of community involvement...and they will act accordingly.

Education

People want to know what is going on in terms of social responsibility. They want to be made aware of ethical, environmental, legal, philanthropic, and money concerns involving organizations; and this can be done if companies use educational practices to create awareness. In the future, there will be no excuse for not educating the general public about social awareness policies, procedures, and happenings. The internet and other social media have made communication to the masses easy and affordable...and leaders of organizations will need to operate with some degree of transparency.

You have almost come to the end of this informative and concise book about social responsibility of organizations. Hopefully, you can use this information whenever and wherever it is needed as you move forward in your personal or professional life. Let's move on to the last section that summarizes everything discussed.

Summary

Social responsibility is gaining importance as organizations try to meet the demands of their customers, the government, and the general public. However, there needs to be a balance between social responsibility and fiduciary responsibility in order to keep everyone happy. This is challenging, but it can be done...and it will need to be done as companies move forward.

This book focuses on social responsibility of organizations by:

- Examining the types of social responsibility
- Evaluating the impact of social responsibility
- Analyzing the advantages of social responsibility
- Exploring the problems of social responsibility
- Suggesting ways for improving social responsibility
- Discussing the future of social responsibility

The text is information and educational, and it is written for easy reader understanding at all levels.

Congratulations! You now understand more about social responsibility in organizations...and increasingly important aspect of conducting business all over the world.

Organizational Ethics
Problems and Solutions

Louis Bevoc

Published by
NutriNiche System LLC

Louis Bevoc books...simple explanations of complex subjects

Definition of organizational ethics

Organizational ethics are formal and informal guidelines designed to regulate employee actions. They describe how people should behave in the workplace and combat employee activities that management deems unacceptable. In short, these guidelines establish ideas of right and wrong and need to be followed because unethical actions set undesirable precedents.

Undesirable precedents can develop in a relatively short period of time, and they can cause multiple problems if they are allowed continue. Employees who witness unethical behavior might assume it is acceptable and start doing it themselves. The end result can be a downward spiral for the organization and the people working in it.

Organizational example

Sarah is a clerical worker who chooses to read novels for personal enjoyment instead of doing her job when the office manager is not in the office. Other clerks see her behavior and also begin to do personal tasks when the boss is away. This prevents necessary office work from being completed in a timely manner and slowly starts negatively affecting other departments in the company.

Workplace ethics are significant because they affect the health and profitability of an organization. They determine proper ways for employees to conduct themselves in specific situations and define ideas of excellence, justice, virtue, right, and wrong. They are important to the organization and the community it resides in.

Organizational example

When employees at a window assembly company eat lunch outside, a few select people choose to leave the trash they create at the company supplied picnic tables instead of putting it in the garbage can. Over time, this creates a wealth of litter in the community, and rats begin to enter the area for an easy food source. People in the neighborhood become upset, and they complain to the city government. The city government has the police department issue the company a fine for improper sanitary conditions. The company pays people to clean up the neighborhood, hires a pest control company to get rid of the rodents, and removes the picnic tables so employees have nowhere to sit if they go outside....all because of a few people's unethical actions.

The above example might not happen exactly as written, but there is little question about the importance of ethics. In fact, in light of the not so distant Wall Street scandals, ethics may now be regarded one of the most significant aspects of any organization. These recognized requirements of right and wrong are related to honesty, loyalty, and commitment, and they are an extension of the organization's values. Those values are like a moral compass that guides the organization toward a foundation of highly effective ideas.

Now that we have defined the meaning of organizational ethics, let's discuss the difference between ethical and unethical behavior.

Determining ethical and unethical behavior

Unethical behavior is not always crystal clear. Some things that appear to be unethical might actually not be...especially when culture comes into play. Bribery, for example, may be considered unethical in the United States, but it is a conventional practice in other nations. In fact, bribes are regularly accepted and largely go unnoticed. Sometimes, they are even expected in order to conduct business, and people are offended if this protocol is not followed. This indicates that there might be times in business when the situation needs to be considered before personal beliefs and/or values.

Values are people's beliefs about conduct that is considered acceptable or good. That being said, **values** of organizations vary greatly based on the goals of those organizations.

Organizational example

A Christian radio station likely would not want employees surfing pornographic websites because this opposes their fundamental beliefs. However, Hustler Magazine might view the same surfing differently because it is "work related." Many people might disagree with Hustler's values from a moral or ethical standpoint, but they tie into the company's organizational objectives.

Organizational objectives are linked to ethical guidelines, and many organizations establish those guidelines in writing. They are used to determine ethical and unethical actions, and they consist of the following:

Employee conduct

Organizations often define acceptable behavior by informing employees in writing how they are expected to conduct themselves. These guidelines address things such as attire (uniforms, suits, casual dress, exposed body parts, etc.), sexual harassment (male or female), and language (profanity, sexual overtones, verbal aggressiveness, etc.). Employees who do not conduct themselves properly are subject to disciplinary action up to and including termination from the organization.

Organizational example

A heating and cooling company requires that all employees wear uniforms when servicing customers. This helps customers feel safe when they let strangers into their homes to service furnaces or air conditioners. It also makes employees believe they are a representative of the organization, and therefore an extension of its image. They understand that they must behave in a certain manner in order to uphold the standards of the organization, and part of that behavior involves acting ethically in people's homes. Damaging properly or leaving a mess after working would not be considered ethical behavior.

Employee accountability

Essentially this involves taking responsibility for actions. Employees need to properly complete the tasks assigned to them in a timely manner. If they experience problems that prevent them from doing this, then they need to contact their supervisor for help. If they do something wrong, then they need own up to it and work toward a resolution in a professional manner. In order for organizational goals to be achieved, employees need to be held accountable for their performance while adhering to established rules and norms.

Organizational example

Susan is an account executive in an advertising agency. She is working on a radio commercial for a client and fears she will not be able to meet the deadline in two days because she has been feeling ill and is unable to think clearly and creatively. Instead of putting out a commercial that is done with minimal effort, she contacts her supervisor and explains the situation. Her supervisor tells her to go home to rest, and he personally finishes the commercial. Susan made an ethical decision to tell her supervisor two days before the deadline so he had time to properly complete the project.

Employee dedication

Strong work ethics and commitment toward organizational goals apply here. Part of that commitment involves attitude because attitude is related to job satisfaction. People who are not satisfied with their jobs tend to be less committed to their organization, and this can affect work behavior, attendance, motivation, and productivity. A positive attitude is also required as inspiration for other employees to remain dedicated.

Organizational example

Lisa is an airline stewardess who is always upbeat and cheerful...even when dealing with customers who are not very happy about being stuck in a seat with limited movement for the next six hours. She is upholding the standards of the airline by remaining positive, and her attitude helps prevent unethical behavior from other employees. In short, Lisa creates an optimistic culture by keeping other employees motivated and out of trouble.

Employee honor

This is likely the most important guideline. Employees need to work with each other to accomplish goals, and this involves honesty and integrity. Withholding information, backstabbing, gossiping, and social loafing all need to be avoided. Work needs to be performed in a timely and professional manner, and professional courtesy needs to be extended to others so they can efficiently and effectively complete their tasks.

Organizational example

Jack is an employee who works in a group at a newspaper publisher. He consistently pushes his responsibilities on other group members, thereby behaving in an unethical manner. He needs to assume a certain responsibility for the group project, and he is not doing this if he chooses instead to be a slacker. If a code of honor was established and written, Jack would not be allowed to behave in this manner.

Unethical behavior of employees

Some employees make bad choices regardless of the guidelines established by the organization. One reason for this is those employees are unsure what to do in certain situations. The ethical dilemma typically seems very apparent once it is discovered and deemed wrong, but making the right choice at the time of occurrence might not have been so obvious.

Organizational example

Ricardo is a delivery person who accepts tickets to a professional basketball game from a customer. The rules state that employees cannot accept any type of gifts, but this is a big customer, and the Ricardo does not want to jeopardize business by turning down the tickets. He takes the tickets even thought he might be endangering his job.

Some employees know what is right and still choose to proceed in the wrong direction. They do this out of self-interest, self-obsession, overzealous ambition, or greed...even though they realize they are violating ethical guidelines of the corporation.

Organizational example

Sam is a buyer of computers who lets a supplier make his house payment in exchange for a big order. This is obviously wrong, but greed is a major factor in Sam's thought process. He only thinks about the purchase in terms of the benefits for himself, and his only worry is getting caught.

The last reason employees behave unethically is the result of misguided communication. People sometimes lie because they think they are being loyal to the organization, even though it will not result in any personal gain.

Organizational example

Wendy is a laboratory technician at a yogurt manufacturer who chooses to hide the pathogenic bacteria findings she detects in the product. She believes she helping the company by making sure the sale is completed and the order is not held up for further analysis. That appears honorable, but if someone gets sick and the product recall is initiated, Wendy might have jeopardized more than just her job. She could be facing jail time for falsifying records that jeopardize the health of the public.

Unethical behavior of organizations

Historically, there have been many different types of unethical behavior in organizations. Corporations have dumped millions of gallons of waste into oceans and waterways, spewed pollution into the air, and left tons of waste in landfills where it does not decompose. Other companies have overcharged the government for health related procedures, overbilled insurance companies, and used tax deductible donations for personal gain of employees.

Unfortunately, these types of unethical and unlawful business methods exist, but why is this so? What are the reasons for the wrong actions committed by these organizations? The answer involves money. It's much less expensive to dump waste in an ocean than it is to have it picked up and properly disposed of, and billing the government for services that were never performed is virtually 100 percent profit. Bribes and payoffs are also easy money that can be generated for long periods of time. As long as both parties involved willingly consent, this unethical activity can go on indefinitely.

Unfortunately, unethical organizations provide a lifestyle that reinforces illicit activities. They even recruit employees who have the same mindset for dishonest behavior, and those employees immediately become an active part of the culture.

Whistleblowers, or people who tell authorities about corporate wrongdoing, are able to stop some unethical issues with their reporting. These individuals can be customers, suppliers, employees, or someone on the streets who witnesses unethical activities. Their work is admirable and justified, but it also involves risk. They stick their necks out, and they can be punished or ostracized by those who are profiting from the wrongful activities. It might seem hard to believe, but whistleblowers are often chastised for doing the right thing...and that prevents many from taking the appropriate action.

Effects of unethical behavior

Unethical actions in the workplace can affect employees and the organizations where they work. There are many problems that can result from this type of dishonesty, so let's examine a few of them.

Legal issues

These include lawsuits, fines, and imprisonment. Organizations that are part of unethical activities might be sued by the affected parties if those parties find that activity detrimental. Nobody wants to be on the receiving end of a lawsuit. Even if they win, they still have to spend money and time proving their innocence. Fines from regulating bodies might also be imposed due to legal issues. If the government determines an organization has violated established rules and regulations pertaining to ethics, there is little they can do to combat the fines levied against them due to the cost involved. Last, and often times most important, employees can go to prison for unethical activity.

Organizational example

The CEO of a corporation faces a jail term because he is aware of unscrupulous activity in the company he oversees and does nothing to stop it.

Public relations issues

The internet and social media spread news very quickly...regardless of whether that news is good or bad. When unethical activities of organizations go public, the perception of that organization becomes negative. This can be a very challenging situation to get out of and that is why big companies spend so much money on public relations campaigns that prevent this type of trouble.

Organizational example

A toy manufacturer is sourcing out all of its work to foreign countries, and it has eliminated thousands of US jobs in the process. When this information reaches the public, they perceive the job elimination as unethical and think of the company in a negative light. This is bad for the company's image, and they need to develop a plan of defense. That defense, however, is very expensive and there is no guarantee that it will be successful. In short, public relations issues involving unethical practices are a nightmare for organizations.

Credibility issues

This problem makes complete sense because any organization that brings negative news upon it due to unethical behavior will lose credibility with the public.

Organizational example

An oil and natural gas company has a large oil spill in a pristine area of ocean off Alaska's coast. This makes some people, especially environmentalists, upset. This problem worsens when the company does not act swiftly and aggressively with their clean-up effort, and the end result is a loss of credibility for the organization. That creditability can be restored, but it will take a lot of money and time, and it could have been avoided if the company had acted responsibly and ethically.

Trust issues

The worst part about losing trust is the fact that it is difficult to restore when the situation involves unethical actions. People can forgive others and learn to trust them again for some wrong doings, but not for those involving ethics.

Organizational example

A financial advisor who loses her home to foreclosure might be able to retain clients because her mistake can be forgiven and she still has investment skills that are of value. However, if that same adviser is involved in a Ponzi scheme, then her clients lose trust that can never be restored.

Productivity issues

Employees who witness unethical behavior in organizations are less committed to that organization. The dishonest activities they observe lower their moral and reduce their respect for the leaders that should be taking control of the problem. Ultimately, they lose motivation, and this lack of motivation results in reduced output.

Organizational example

Sales people see their boss charging his personal expenses to the company, even though their expense accounts are monitored very closely. This unethical behavior de-motivates the sales staff as they question why executive management lets their boss get away with action that is obviously wrong. They react by doing less work themselves and remaining bitter at the management for their lack of response.

Preventing unethical employee behavior

As you are now aware, unethical activities pose many problems for employees and organizations. These problems are often difficult to rectify once they are ingrained in the culture, so the best way to avoid them is to implement a prevention strategy. When it comes to organizational ethics, "failing to plan is planning to fail."

The following are some ideas that can be used for prevention:

Implement training

Proper training is a must for prevention of unwanted behavior. Quite frankly, employees cannot be held accountable for behaving a certain way if they have not been taught the difference between right and wrong. They can use the "nobody ever told me" excuse when they are not meeting organizational expectations, and the end result can be problematic.

Organizational example

Randy is a recently hired bank teller who has never been shown how to properly balance his drawer at the end of the day. He has a good idea how to balance using the bank's standard procedure, but it is faster and easier to do it another way.

At the end of one particular work week, the bank manager Jennifer discovers that Randy's drawer was not properly balanced for four of the past five days. She is upset because this tarnishes her work record and will look bad to bank executives when she applies for her next promotion. Jennifer tells Randy that he needs to be more diligent and follow company procedures. He responds that he was never trained on company procedure and did not know he was doing anything wrong.

There is nothing Jennifer can do in terms of reprimanding because she did not conduct any training. Randy actually was aware of how to balance his drawer properly, but he committed unethical behavior because it was easy and convenient, and he knew he had an excuse if he was caught making mistakes. This would have never happened if he had been properly trained at the beginning of his employment.

Establish objectives

This involves setting goals so employees have something legitimate to strive towards. Goals help them stay focus on designated tasks and avoid potential trouble elsewhere. Two things, however, need to be considered when setting these goals. First, make sure the goals are attainable. Employees who need to meet goals that are unreachable might resort to unethical actions to accomplish their objectives. Second, make sure employee process is monitored. Employees who are mot monitored become unmotivated and often lack efficiency to complete designated tasks.

Organizational example

Corporate management at a health store chain tells employees they have a goal to sell 20 bottles of multivitamins per week in every store. Nobody in management checks the progress of the employees for six weeks, and when they do, they find that sales are only averaging 11 bottles per store. Management also reviews the store cameras and finds employees talking to friends at the store instead of serving customers. Because the employees' progress was not monitored, they chose the unethical action of talking to friends instead of trying to achieve their designated goal. The goal was obtainable, but the process was not followed up on properly.

Establish a code of conduct

A written conduct code provides employees specific guidelines on how they are expected to behave at work. It describes activities that are desirable and undesirable, and it details actions that will be taken if the code is violated.

Organizational example

Thomas is an employee in a pet store who likes to show off to customers. Specifically, he pulls a parrot from its cage and entices it to say funny things. The customers and his friends think this act is funny, but it is not something that Brenda the owner would approve of if she knew it was happening.

One day, while attempting to pull the parrot from the cage, Thomas knocks it off the perch and injures it. Two days later, the bird dies. Brenda is upset, but there is little she can do because she has never established written rules on employee animal handling. Thomas' behavior was unethical and resulted in a bird's death, but this situation would not have transpired if a code of conduct was in place.

Lead by example

This one is easy. Managers need to follow rules and regulations of the organization if they want to maintain an ethical workplace. If they utilize a "do as I say, not as I do" mentality, they will violate the trust of their employees. Trust is critical in an organization because employees who trust management are more faithful, and faithful employees are less likely to act unethically.

Organizational example

Larry is a cruise ship captain. The parent company of the cruise ship has a strict rule that employees are not allowed to enter guest rooms without the guests being present. However, on several occasions, employees have witnessed Larry entering guest's rooms without their knowledge. He has the right to do this if he suspects illegal activity, but he has told some workers that he is simply curious about what he might find.

Larry's behavior results in the employees loosing trust in him and faith in their organization, and they ultimately are not concerned about following other rules established by the parent company. This would not have happened if Larry had led by example and followed the rules.

Hire outside experts

Most organizations specialize in selling products or services that are part of their core business. Typically, that core business does not involve unethical behavior prevention. That being said, organizations that are not proficient in preventing unethical behavior still need expertise in that area, and that expertise can be obtained by hiring outside companies as consultants.

Organizational example

A company hires George, an experienced consultant and speaker, to talk about organizational ethics. He discusses ethical and unethical behavior and, through example, indicates their importance in the workplace. He also explains that the type of industry, size of company, or market share percentage does not matter when it comes to ethics because unethical behavior can happen in any organization regardless of their magnitude or structure. He also uses video, handouts, and role-playing to show the significance of organizational ethics and prevent employees from making bad choices.

Create Checks and Balances

One thing that all organizations can learn from a truly democratic government is that checks and balances are needed to prevent inappropriate actions from people at all levels. Organizations that put all responsibilities in the hands of one person or small group of people are at risk for unethical behavior.

Organizational example

Think about an automotive dealership where a salesperson sells the car, a credit analyst authorizes the sale, a cashier rings up the purchase, and an accountant makes certain the receivables are properly documented. If one person was in charge of all of these transactions, then there would be no checks in place and it would open the door for that individual to act unethically.

Establish hiring procedures

Organizations need to put time and effort into the employee selection process because new employees can affect the overall ethical environment. This process should include background checks, education verification, and employment history confirmation because people that cheat and lie bring their unethical behavior into the cultures where they are employed.

Organizational example

Penny, a candidate for an accounts payable position, states that she has a master's degree from a reputable university. Upon verification of this claim, it is found that she only has an undergraduate degree and was kicked out of graduate school for repeated plagiarism. If she cheated on his course work and lied about a degree, then she might be an ethical risk as an accountant and the organization should not hire her.

Summary

The importance of ethical employee behavior cannot be over emphasized. It affects the image, status, stability, and profitability of organizations, and it damages people's careers. Unethical activities are so critical that severe instances can lead to the destruction of organizations and time spent in jail for the violators.

Unethical actions in organizations reach far beyond the workers and managers employed within. They influence the local community, bring about legal issues, violate trust, and affect the image of the organization worldwide if it competes globally. The resulting damage is difficult to rectify and the costs involved are astronomical.

The best way to personally prevent unethical dilemmas is to think before you act. Don't risk jeopardizing your livelihood or creating a dark cloud that will follow you for the rest of your career by making a poor ethical choice. In short, avoid becoming an example that someone uses in a future book on unethical behavior.

Nonprofit Organizations

A Basic Introduction

Louis Bevoc

Published by
NutriNiche System LLC

Louis Bevoc books...simple explanations of complex subjects

Introduction

Many people start businesses in order to generate income. They sell goods or services to make money as a reward for the time and effort they invest in their livelihood. These businesses are designed to earn profits, and they are regulated by the government based on their for profit status.

A nonprofit organization (NPO) is not the same as a for profit company. NPOs generate income, but that income is not for the investors, shareholders, owners, or employees. The money left after bills are paid is reinvested back into the efforts of the organization. In other words, it helps the organization maintain its status and promote its cause. NPOs are regulated by the government based on their nonprofit status, and they must serve the public in some manner.

NPOs are specifically classified as such by the Internal Revenue Service (IRS). This means they are granted tax-exempt status and usually money donated to them is tax deductible. Additionally, all financial information is required to be made public so anyone who donates can see how their money is being used.

Workforces of NPOs are generally established for humanitarian, environmental, freedom, or religious reasons. They further a cause by promoting an idea, belief, or concept that appeals to people's emotional or spiritual needs rather than a product or service that has value in a specific market. Unlike for profit operations, NPOs rely on donations and grants from individuals, organizations, and governments.

NPO workers are rewarded differently than employees in for profit companies. For profit businesses financially compensate the vast majority of their employees, and people work at these organizations so they can earn a living. NPOs have limited numbers of paid employees with most people volunteering their time and effort. These individuals identify with the cause of the NPO, tend to work tirelessly, and their reward is the success of the organization. Since the volunteers work for free, they are generally never fired. If they stop working for the cause, it is usually by their own choice.

This book focuses on nonprofit organizations. It explores types, economic influences, advantages, disadvantages, trends, and the future of this business concept. The text is informational and educational, and it is written for easy understanding at any reader level.

Please note that this book does not discuss specific legalities of NPOs. It touches upon their tax status, but it is not intended to be used as a legal reference for those who are considering opening or are involved with nonprofit businesses. It does not go into any detail on issues such as the tax exempt requirements, tax deduction of donations, or the sub listing of 501(c) classifications. People interested in the legalities of NPOs should read books that are geared toward that subject.

Now that you understand the scope of this book, let's move on to the next section that examines specific types of NPOs.

Types

It would be very difficult to list every type of NPO because they vary so much in composition and cause. However, the major types are listed below.

Advocacy

These groups are the most political of the different types. They have a goal in mind, and they will generally do whatever is necessary to achieve that goal. Sometimes their goal is to influence people so they make choices that reflect the group's effort, and other times it is to change or repeal something that is already in effect. Often known as political action committees or special interest groups, advocacy NPOs lobby hard using supporter funds to achieve their objectives.

One problem with advocacy NPOs is they sometimes resort to illegal activities to achieve goals and objectives. They are so intent on furthering their cause that they have been known to commit crimes including bribery and fraud. They also get involved in non-violent activities (also known as civil obedience) to bring attention to the ideas supported by their organizations.

Association

These NPOs are organized in order to bring people together who share a common interest. That interest can be education (parent-teacher associations), experience (war veterans), finance (credit unions), lifestyle (condominium associations) or something secretive (masons). Associations often involve rituals or other activities unique to the people in the NPO. For example, fraternities (educational associations) sometimes have a handshake that is used to greet and identify brothers. The handshake is only divulged after a person becomes a member....and it is not to be discussed or used with any non-members.

Charity

Charitable NPOs collect money for select causes. Many times this is for health concerns (muscular dystrophy), catastrophic circumstance (earthquake), social inequality (foundations), or animal protection (animal shelters). These organizations are almost entirely funded by outside donations, and they have extremely dedicated personnel.

One problem associated with charitable NPOs in the fact that that part of the money received is spent on overhead and marketing costs. This portion of revenue varies depending on the organization, but some people believe that not enough goes to the designated cause. This is not necessarily illegal, but it does bring about ethical concerns.

Cooperative

Cooperative NPOs are formed when people work together to achieve common good for everyone involved (such as the Dairy Farmers of America). Farmers often form cooperatives for financial reasons such as lowering the seed prices for crops or raising the quality of feed for animals. The power of these individuals functioning as a unit benefits everyone in that unit. These NPOs are typically funded by members or outside donations from individuals, organizations, or the government (in the form of grants).

Recreation and socialization

These NPOs include country clubs, hiking groups, and hobbyists. The form when people seek others who share common recreational, personal, or social interests in order further those interests. Members typically want to obtain knowledge, add to their collection, socialize, exercise, or relax. They might meet at someone's home, a sports facility, or an outdoor park. However, regardless of where they meet, they do it for mutual interest reasons. An example is a chess club that rents out library space for monthly tournaments or a bike club that meets at a designated destination to ride for a pre-determined number of miles.

The biggest positive about recreation and socialization NPOs is the fact that money is not typically a concern. They are almost always funded by the members themselves, and those members usually work somewhere else to earn money in order to make a living. They have expendable income that they voluntarily give to the NPO, and they become part of it for enjoyment purposes rather than furthering some type of cause. For this reason, they do not need to be continually contacted for donations by those who do the organizing.

Religious

Religious NPOs are quite common in America...partially due to the separation of church and state reference in the *First Amendment to the Constitution of the United States* that allows for freedom of religion. These organizations unite members of specific faiths for spiritual purposes, and they are often self-funded. The Jonah Project is an example of this type of NPO.

Unfortunately, these types of NPOs come under scrutiny by the government due to the fact that the financial aspects involved can be abused. High ranking members sometimes compensate themselves rather than putting the money back into the organization to further its cause.

Now you understand some of the major types of NPOs. However, classification goes a step further because some of these organizations are public (for example credit unions) while others are private (for example home associations). Since these two categories make a difference in operating strategies, private and public NPOs are discussed in the next section.

Public vs. Private

Each type of NPO can be further classified as public or private. The major difference between the two is that public NPOs receive donations from the general public, while private NPOs received financial backing from a few select contributors.

The following is a more detailed description of public and private NPOs:

Public

As noted above, public NPOs receive funding from the general public. They offer perks for certain types of paid memberships, such as discounts on products or services from organizations that also support the NPO. In this situation, one hand essentially washes the other and both parties feel good about contributing to a noteworthy cause.

An example of a public NPO is St. Jude Children's Research hospital started by Danny Thomas in 1962. This charitable organization has received donations from people and organizations all over the world. American Lebanese Syrian Associated Charities (ALSAC), another non-profit charity, is responsible for fundraising of the Children's hospital that totals almost 2 million dollars per day. Obviously, this amount of money would be difficult to collect from a few select donors, and that is one reason why St. Jude is a public NPO.

Private

As noted above, private NPOs are funded from a few select sources. In fact, some small private NPOs are entirely funded by one wealthy donor who is interested bringing attention to the cause. These types of organizations usually do not look for contributions from the general public, but that could change if the need arises. Private NPOs also have lower operating costs than their public counterparts because far less money is spent on marketing or fundraising activities. This is advantageous because a higher percentage of each dollar is used directly for the cause, and it is a reason why some people choose support private rather than public NPOs.

As you can see, public and private NPOs differ in the ways that they are funded. However, both types of organizations have a goal of furthering the cause for which they were established. Next, let's looks at the advantages and disadvantages offered by all types of NPOs...starting with the advantages.

Advantages

NPOs offer many different advantages. Some of these advantages are external and visual, such as the ability to solicit funding from individuals who believe in a specific cause; and some of them are internal and less transparent, such as the satisfaction those individuals receive from giving.

To simplify matters, NPO advantages are broken down as follows:

Identification

NPOs all have some type of cause, and they receive funding because people or organizations identify with that cause. Interestingly, that identification is for different reasons. For example, three different people donate money to an NPO that services the needs of war veterans. The first person donates because her father and grandfather were war veterans. The second person donates because he has read that veterans often do not receive proper medical care. The third person donates because he wants a tax deduction and helping veterans seems like a noble cause. The reasons for each of these individual donations are not the same, but the all believe they are giving to a worthwhile cause. In short, each of these individuals identifies with war veterans and finds it advantageous to give to them.

Variety

Variety is often thought of as the spice of life...and that type of thinking can also be applied to people's jobs. After all, they spend a large percentage of their waking day at work, so their jobs should have variety in order to make them interesting.

People who work for NPOs experience a great deal of variety. In fact, the diverse nature of their responsibilities often makes their work more enjoyable than any other job they have ever done. They are usually assigned to multiple projects at the same time, and these projects allow them to make decisions on a moment's notice. This provides ample opportunity for growth...the type of growth that is simply not possible in many for profit organizations.

In short, NPOs are not looking for specialists who prefer one specific type of job responsibility. They search for people who like to multi task and enjoy new challenges...a type of environment where opportunities for learning are virtually endless.

Communication

This is an advantage that many people, including NPO employees, do not readily recognize. Workers at NPOs regularly get to discuss organizational happens with the top people or person in the organization. This is due to the fact that NPOs usually have flat hierarchies with one or two levels of management. Heads of these organizations do not distance themselves from the rank and file employees, and this makes communication much better. Unfortunately, the same cannot be said for many for profit organizations where CEOs are never found meeting or socializing with lower level employees.

Commitment

People who work for NPOs find a lot of satisfaction, regardless of whether they receive compensation or volunteer. They are supporting a cause they view as justifiable and necessary, and this makes them feel good about their efforts. When they feel good about their efforts, they identify with the organization and its goals...and this helps the organization function more efficiently and effectively. In short, NPO employees are committed to their workplaces thereby creating a win-win situation for employees and organizations.

Knowledge

Contrary to what some people in for profit businesses believe, NPOs place a very high priority on business skills. They search for people who believe in the cause and have worked in for profit organizations so they can tap their minds for the knowledge within. When these individuals are brought on board, they combine their strengths to make the NPO the best it can be in regard to accomplishing goals and objectives. Smart leaders of NPOs recognized the need for knowledge, and they know it can be found in the for profit sector.

The advantages of NPOs are many, but there are also some associated disadvantages. These disadvantages typically do not discourage organizations from becoming or remaining non-profit, but they do exist...and they are discussed in the next section

Disadvantages

As most people who have worked for NPOs understand, there are disadvantages for these types of organizations. Similar to advantages, some disadvantages are external and visual, such as the technology that is available for people to do their jobs. However, other disadvantages are not as easily seen, such as the frustration experienced by workers or volunteers who cannot see themselves making progress toward furthering the cause.

To simplify matters, NPO disadvantages are broken down as follows:

Frustration

One NPO disadvantage is the fact that it can be difficult to pinpoint progress or achievement on a small scale. For example, a group of animal rights activists are picketing outside of a store that sells mink coats. After the store owner calls the police, they are forced to leave the properly...and this raises questions. Did they have any success with their actions? Were they noticed? These questions are hard to answer because it is difficult to determine if anyone was impacted by the picketing. This can be demoralizing to the picketers unless they realize that their efforts are for the greater good of the cause. In other words, it can be challenging for these individuals to look past their immediate situation to see the success of the organization as a whole....and this can be frustrating.

Technology

This disadvantage can be minimal or substantial based on the importance of technology to the NPO. If state of the art technology plays a big role in furthering the cause, then this disadvantage can be paralyzing. For example, sophisticated software might be necessary for an NPO to implement data, track trends, formulate reports, and determine course of action. However, that software can be expensive...especially if it needs to be continually updated. Since the NPO relies on donations to operate, that money might simply not be available. This prevents them from reaching the level that they need to be in order to complete their designated goals and objectives, and it could lead to failing to secure the funding necessary to continue their efforts in the future.

Funding

Funding controls every NPO, and donors are the sole source of that funding. Contributors who decide not to donate can stop an NPO dead in its tracks. This is similar to for profit organizations relying on sales, but donors are usually much scarcer than customers. For profit businesses can diversity their customer bases to include a variety of outlets for their products or services. NPOs usually do not have this opportunity because only a select few people or organizations have an interest in their cause.

Additionally, there is a constant need for NPOs to solicited funding. Customers of for profit organizations often return without prompting because they like the product or service they have purchased. However, this is rarely the case for NPOs. If donors are not contacted, then they often choose not to donate again. They need to be reminded of their importance to the organization and the importance of the organization's cause to those impacted by it. This means time and effort must be continually dedicated to fundraising, and that takes away from doing other work that furthers the cause of the NPO.

Structure

As noted in the advantages sections, communication in NPOs is often better than that in for profit organizations because much of the management is done at ground level without the multiple layers organizational hierarchy found in many companies. Unfortunately, this type of organizational structure is not all good. A major negative associated with it is the fact that there is no leadership at lower levels to implement the plans made by higher ranking personnel. Every rank and file employee has essentially the same amount of authority, and this can result in nobody taking charge. More importantly, it can lead to internal conflict over who has authority. If that conflict becomes dysfunctional, then personal attacks can result where the combatants focus on position rather than principal...and nothing constructive gets accomplished.

In a nutshell, for profit organizations typically have lower levels of managers that are in charge of departments, teams, or groups. This allows tasks to be delegated to subordinate levels of authority so they implement and complete them. NPOs, on the other hand, are flat when it comes to management. This is understandable due to cost factors, but it also hinders goals and objectives from getting accomplished. When goals and objectives are not accomplished, NPOs are unable to further their cause...and this makes people think twice about donating their hard-earned money.

Turnover

Turnover is a concern for many different types of organizations, but it is particularly threatening for NPOs. This is due to the fact that NPOs have a special set of factors that do not apply to profit based entities.

Turnover factors for NPOs are as follows:

Safety

For example, a man who works for a forest preservation NPO has his life threatening by loggers who make a living harvesting lumber from trees. He determines his efforts are not worth the potential consequences, so he stops volunteering for the NPO.

Second thoughts

For example, a man who works for a forest preservation realizes that native people in isolated areas cannot feed their families without hunting wild game and gathering fruits from the forest. He decides that he cannot consciously tell these people to discontinue their current way of life, so he chooses to stop volunteering for the NPO.

Pressure

For example, a man who works for a forest preservation NPO dreads calling people and asking them for their financial support. These people have told the man to quit calling, but the head of the NPO tells him to continue doing so because the funding is desperately needed. He reaches a point where he simply cannot make another solicitation phone call, so he chooses to stop volunteering for the NPO.

Now you understand some advantages and disadvantages of NPOs. Let's expand on the discussion by examining the impact that the economy on these organizations. This is an interesting subject because some of this impact is not as transparent as it might appear at first glance.

Economic impact

Most people know that the economy has an impact on for profit businesses. When the economy gets worse, people tend to forego unnecessary expenses and many businesses are negatively affected. These businesses see reduced sales resulting in less profit and, in worst case scenarios, this leads to their demise.

The economy also has an impact on NPOs. In fact, this impact is often bigger than that on for profit businesses because NPOs are hit twice as hard. Please consider the following as support:

For profit organizations

If the economy is bad, then sales for many different types of businesses start to decline. This is due to the fact that people have less expendable income so they limit their spending to essential goods and services. Organizations that suffer the worst include restaurants and companies involved in the vacation business because people tend to eat at home and avoid going on trips in order to save money. Sales decline as demand for the products and services decrease and some organizations end up in financially troubling situations.

When the economy is good, for profit organizations tend to do better. The demand for their products and services increases because people have extra money that they are not afraid to use for items that are not necessarily essential. This leads to businesses becoming profitable, and they are able to grow and prosper.

NPOs

Some NPOs are hit with a double whammy when the economy sours. People have less expendable income...and financial support for a cause is typically one of the first things to go. This is understandable because NPO support is a non-essential expenditure. However, many times the demand for NPO services increases as donor contributions decrease. For example, the services of an NPO that feeds the hungry and shelters the homeless will be needed more as the economy tanks and people lose jobs. However, there is now less money to support those services...and that lack of funding prevents them from achieving their objectives. Obviously, this is not the case for every NPO. The demand for the services offered by other types of NPOs does not necessarily increase as the economy gets bad, but donations still decrease...and this means the NPOs have less money available to continue working at the same level.

When the economy is good, NPOs are at a peak for productivity. They get more donations because people are not afraid to give their money to a cause that they deem worthwhile. Additionally, fewer people are out of work so there is less need for services that help people during difficult times. Along the same lines, the demand for the work done by other types of NPOs typically does not necessarily increase, but the additional money from funding allows them to do more to further their causes.

Now you are aware of the impact the economy has on NPOs and the reasons it affects them differently than for profit organizations. With this in mind, let's move forward into the next section that discusses the things NPOs need to do in future in order to weather economic storms, promote their cause, and reach new levels of growth.

Future

This section deserves some attention because NPOs will need to change in the future in order to thrive and survive. The following gives some insight into the type of changes that will take place:

Results driven investments

In many ways, people who give to NPOs are "investing" their hard-earned money in those organizations. Yes, they believe in the cause or they would not be supporting it. However, like other investments, they write a check and monitor the performance of that investment. In NPOs, that performance is usually determined by accomplishments that show results. As might be expected, those results are analyzed and the donor makes a decision on whether he or she wants to "reinvest" in the future.

Results have always been important to donors, but that importance is going to increase substantially in the future. NPOs will be compared against each other to determine which ones are performing best in the minds of those contributing. Results, rather than cause, will be the biggest factor determining the destination of expendable income.

Educated donors

Donors will conduct research on the NPOs that receive their contributions. Social media and the internet have made this relatively easy, and the use of these tools will increase in the future because donors will be very comfortable with technology. This increased level of education will mean that donors will become more selective about which organizations receive their contributions. They will not give less money, but the money they contribute will need to be justified by the NPOs receiving it.

Increased staff

People will realize that the infrastructure of NPOs is important in order to run those organizations effectively. Funds will be put aside to hire management personnel who are in charge of completing tasks, and this will not be frowned upon by donors. In fact, donors will realize the value of management and contribute even more money. Unfortunately, this will not be all positive because hierarchical charts will increase causing a lack of communication. Also, the percentage of volunteers will likely decrease...and sometimes volunteers are the most dedicated personnel because they believe most in the cause.

Narrowed marketing

NPOs will realize that they have a specific market that provides them with most of their funding. That being said, they will focus on that specific market and move away from trying to entice others in the population to donate. Marketing money will largely be spent on the renewal of current donors rather than the search for new people willing to contribute.

Marketing money will also be spent on corporate donor solicitation. Corporate giving is important for public image, and CEOs are beginning to take advantage this fact. They will donate more money to charitable causes in the future in order to establish credibility in the eyes of consumers. In short, the leaders of companies will utilize NPOs as their own marketing tool, and this means that corporate giving has only begun to reach its full potential.

Competition

This refers to the competition between NPOs for the funding that is available. It takes into account the thinking that people will become more educated and organizational leaders will work toward establishing positive perceptions of companies. All donors will be looking for "more bang for their buck," and this means competition between NPOs will increase. NPOs will need to find ways to stand out from the rest of the pack in order to get the funding necessary to further their causes. This is possible, but it will take creative thinking and hard work. Unfortunately, NPOs that fail to distinguish themselves from the competition will likely dissolve.

Expect the unexpected

Every company needs to expect the unexpected, but this thinking is more applicable to NPOs than it is to most other organizations. NPOs are scrutinized by the public and governmental agencies for ethical and legal reasons, and this means the laws regulating them could change at any time. NPO leaders need to be ready for this with strategies that can be used to maintain status and continue furthering causes under a variety of different circumstances. In short, NPOs need to plan because those that "fail to plan, plan to fail"

Summary

NPOs can be found all over the United States. They further specific causes, are funded by donors that support those causes, and sometimes have an impact worldwide.

This book focuses on NPOs. It explores specific types, investigates advantages and disadvantages, analyzes the economy's impact, and discusses the future of these businesses. The text is informational and educational, and it is written for easy reader understanding at all levels.

Congratulations! You now understand more about the nonprofit organizations that play a critical role in bringing attention to important causes.